Telephone Tips

by Marcus Jones

Scott Foresman
is an imprint of

Glenview, Illinois • Boston, Massachusetts • Mesa, Arizona
Shoreview, Minnesota • Upper Saddle River, New Jersey

Every effort has been made to secure permission and provide appropriate credit for photographic material. The publisher deeply regrets any omission and pledges to correct errors called to its attention in subsequent editions.

Unless otherwise acknowledged, all photographs are the property of Pearson.

Photo locations denoted as follows: Top (T), Center (C), Bottom (B), Left (L), Right (R), Background (Bkgd)

Cover: ©Rob Lewine/Corbis; 3 ©Bettmann/Corbis; 4 ©Corbis; 5 ©Rob Lewine/Corbis; 6 ©Tom Stewart/Corbis; 8 ©Reuters/Corbis

ISBN 13: 978-0-328-39347-3
ISBN 10: 0-328-39347-9

1 2 3 4 5 6 7 8 9 10 V010 17 16 15 14 13 12 11 10 09 08

Alexander Bell and his telephone

Alexander Bell built a telephone in 1876. He had to learn a lot of science to do it.

Here are some telephones from long ago. Do these early phones look like your phone?

Phones use electricity to send calls. Some calls are sent through wires. Some calls are sent through the air.

Some phones can get calls that travel through air.

Using the phone is a great way to talk to friends and family.

Who do you like to talk to on the phone?

The phone can be used to get help when someone is sick.

Using a phone is a big help if there is trouble or danger. For example, if you saw someone get hurt, you or a grown-up would dial 9-1-1.

Dial 9-1-1 to get help.

The people who answer the phone at 9-1-1 will send help. Use your head. Tell them what the problem is. Do not hang up because they need to find out where you are.

Are the roads open after a snowstorm?
Use the telephone to find out.

The telephone is also good for finding things out. For example, you can call your school and find out if it is open after a storm.

Telephones make our lives better.